THE PORTAGE POETRY SERIES

Series Titles

Naming the Ghost
Emily Hockaday

Mourning
Dokubo Melford Goodhead

Messengers of the Gods: New and Selected Poems
Kathryn Gahl

After the 8-Ball
Colleen Alles

Careful Cartography
Devon Bohm

Broken On the Wheel
Barbara Costas-Biggs

Sparks and Disperses
Cathleen Cohen

Holding My Selves Together: New and Selected Poems
Margaret Rozga

Lost and Found Departments
Heather Dubrow

Marginal Notes
Alfonso Brezmes

The Almost-Children
Cassondra Windwalker

Meditations of a Beast
Kristine Ong Muslim

Praise for
Emily Hockaday

"In Emily Hockaday's stirring debut, *Naming the Ghost*, beauty and terror are never far apart. They appear like strangely familiar eyes gleaming through a child-proof window. 'A temptation is not always/a desire. Right? Sometimes it is the darkest fear.' Otherworldly, yet grounded in the dailyness of young motherhood—in baby wipes and brownie mix and queen-sized marital beds—the poems in this collection haunt and delight. They awaken the senses. They remind me that we are never, for better or worse, alone."

—Jared Harél, author of *Go Because I Love You*

"*Naming the Ghost* is a powerhouse of small, intense, sometimes brutal, always brilliant poems about a new mother who is (perhaps) experiencing post partum depression or simply old-fashioned depression. Either way, this amazing collage of poems tells a difficult story. Individual lines are memorable, quotable—'My life is open to autopsy' is only one of many. You can read it all at once (I did) or go through it slowly (as I will later), but either way it will leave a mark."

—Jane Yolen, author of *Kaddish*
Sophie Brody Medal winner

"Emily Hockaday's debut collection, *Naming the Ghost*, is an immersive and unflinching gaze into the relationship between grief, motherhood, and loss. Finding revelation in the mundane, Hockaday's poems reverberate with the tension—and journey—toward healing."

—Diana Marie Delgado, author of *Tracing the Horse*

Naming
the
Ghost

Poems by

Emily Hockaday

Cornerstone Press
Stevens Point, Wisconsin

Cornerstone Press, Stevens Point, Wisconsin 54481
Copyright © 2022 Emily Hockaday
www.uwsp.edu/cornerstone

Printed in the United States of America by
Point Print and Design Studio, Stevens Point, Wisconsin 54481

Library of Congress Control Number: 2022936975
ISBN: 979-8-9861447-0-2

Cornerstone Press titles are produced in courses and internships offered by the
Department of English at the University of Wisconsin–Stevens Point.

DIRECTOR & PUBLISHER   EXECUTIVE EDITOR
Dr. Ross K. Tangedal   Jeff Snowbarger

SENIOR EDITORS
Lexie Neeley, Monica Swinick, Kala Buttke

PRESS STAFF
Rhiley Block, Alyssa Bronk, Grace Dahl, Patrick Fogarty, Ava Freeman, Angela
Green, Brett Hill, Cale Jacoby, Hunter Keisow, Adam King, Jeremy Kremser, Amanda
Leibham, Leo McEvilly, Abbi Wasielewski, Abbi Rohde

For my father, Bruce Hockaday,
and my daughter, Avery Hockaday-Carey,
who overlapped on this Earth for four short months.

Also by Emily Hockaday:

Beach Vocabulary
Space on Earth
Ophelia: A Botanist's Guide
What We Love and Will Not Give Up
Starting a Life

Poems

Naming
the
Ghost

The Ghost Is Here

We know the ghost is here
when we see the pool of water
seeping from under the counter
and the baby's monitor turns on
through the night, static,
and we hear the mourning dove
at our window at midnight.
We greet each other with stoic
silence. We discuss the weather,
check the baby's head
for supernatural heat;
I place the back of my finger
behind her ear—nothing reassures me.
The air is alive. At night
when our ankles touch
under the sheets, I look
at your eyes in the dark,
and they are wet reflective pools—
I see the ghost. I know you see
the same thing in mine.

When the Ghost Speaks

When the ghost speaks
it is the sound of music heard
from under water. And the words
are a forgotten symphony
we composed as children.
My daughter is writing her own
ghost music on her plastic, five-note piano.
My husband doesn't hear it,
but he sees me and the baby listening.
The way we pause, cocking our heads.
He sees the resemblance in the curve
of our necks. In how we can both be looking
at and through him at the same time.
I didn't know we'd be living with this,
he confesses to me, at night. *No one did,*
I say. What he means is that he wouldn't
have chosen it. I make my hands
a soft web and press them against
his face. He is tired. We are all tired.

The Ghost's Warm Breath

Though it is winter and chilly today,
the wind is the ghost's warm breath.
At night the baby coughs like a seal barking;
the doctor calls it croup, but I ask myself:
what is it? I stay up listening, trying
to answer. The ghost orders brownie mix
and baby wipes and socks—
the packages come the very same day.
I ask about my father who is dead
more than a year now, while I peer into
the bare wood of Forest Park hoping
to see the banded face of a raccoon.
When I lay the baby down,
pulling the crocheted blanket
up to her neck at night, I say
I love you. I don't always know
what is speaking.

Unlike My Husband

Unlike my husband,
the ghost can see pain. My nerves glow
red like irons in a fire. Sometimes I wonder
if the ghost sees me at all—is it just the shape
of aching that attracts it? Days when
the last leaves are blown from the trees, curved
like bodies protecting something precious, I dare
a gust to take me, too. The pain makes me in turns
very heavy and then light. I could drift off
the planet, a fine vibration, a whisper,
an exhalation. Something holds me
here, where I belong, with my family
and its laughter. A temptation is not always
a desire. Right? Sometimes it is the darkest fear.

The Ghost Has Started Reading

The ghost has started reading to our daughter
in the night. We find books like *I'll Love You Forever*
and *Runaway Bunny* open and stacked
next to her crib. These are the books
I can never get through; icicles from childhood
that lodged between my ribs and still, in adulthood,
haven't melted. The ghost doesn't perceive temperature.
I look in my daughter's eyes for signs
of frozen shards. When she laughs, is it quieter?
She squirms from my scrutiny with narrow eyes.
Don't you have the story wrong? I ask.
I write a response in the bathroom mirror:
It isn't always about you.

The Ghost Casts a Spell

We set up humidifiers in each room.
We are drying out. Baby waves her hand
through the visible stream of vapor. The ghost
casts a spell over the window so it always appears sunny;
we are exhausted by the anemic winter light.
I sit down with a pen and paper
and write a long letter about nursing
and the feel of letdown in the breasts;
the stitches along my perineum; the feeling
of a full uterus during orgasm. In the morning,
the handwritten page is unmoved. While the others sleep,
I burn it, mix the ashes with potting soil,
and add it to the pots along the window.

Now That We Know

Now that we know about the ghost, I apologize
to my husband; it is no longer his fault
that all of the baby socks are mismatched.
The noises in the pipes that I asked him to look at
may not have existed, and the chronically empty
ice cube tray is explained. So many things
are out of control. People rely on me;
I thought I could rely on people. The ghost is not here
to make me doubt myself. I check the burners
throughout the day and manage to forget
when we rush out the door. I haven't seen a cockroach
in over a year—who do I thank? It is almost Valentine's Day
and I send a care package to my mother, recently widowed.
I agonize over the contents, not wanting to unearth her grief.

The Ghost Knows

The ghost knows it is my fault, but still
enters my dreams as my mother,
saying: *this isn't your fault.*
I'm looking for someone in a crowd,
and when it has dispersed, I can't remember
who I lost. Backs are moving away from me
in all directions. No one
faces me. I wake to the sound
of the mourning doves, and this time,
actually, it is morning. The baby is awake
but entertaining herself in the crib.
Sometimes over the baby monitor, I see it.
Something is out of place. The baby turns
and looks right at the camera, babbling.

Lying in Bed

Lying in bed, fear pinches the base of my skull
to keep me awake. My husband is rolled
away from me, facing the open window.
The cold winter wind feels gentle;
being in bed with the ghost is hot hot hot.
Today the Mars rover Opportunity
was declared dead. This lonely robot
succumbed to one final sandstorm
after years of defiance. Did I ever dream
of going to Mars? Everything is different
when you're dead. Suddenly Mars
might not be Mars at all.

Wake the Ghost

I throw my daughter into the air
and her peals of laughter
wake the worry always lurking
in my blood. Today the ghost is effervescent
as fear, and my daughter's eyes are half moons
of delight. The ghost is made stronger
by adrenaline; it is one too many glasses
of red wine. I hold the baby in a gentle hug,
and she slips between my limbs
like a mouse flattening itself
through a floorboard. Watch how deftly
the baby evades my affection.

I Held the Ghost

Nursing my daughter, I didn't know it,
but the ghost was already with me.
The water I drank wasn't water but the ghost.
The more I drank the thirstier I became.
And the look on the baby's face—
the more I loved the less love I needed.
I was turning into love; I held the baby
and my doubt; I gave them sustenance.
The ghost was trying to teach me about need.
About the right and wrong way to love.

The Ghost Is Water

My father's death has shaken my mortality
loose. Within me it sifts down like salt,
and my sanity is water. They say these are
the building blocks of life; I alternate between feeling
electrically alive and disassociated. Let my fear
fall away like petals. Let my body show its colors
and choose what to do with me after all. Am I
permitted to stay here? With this baby
and my spouse? The ghost lurks outside the window
tonight, a haze around the full glow of the moon.

The Ghost Flies Low

It flies low overhead like airplanes landing at JFK
when it's overcast. My husband suggests strategies
on how to deal with this. *Have you let it into your body?*
I ask him. The baby only draws in purple. Purple curls
over and over like the shape of a curved spine or the letter C
or the ghost. We move her drawings around on the floor,
looking for the right combination to decipher the message
or link the code. *I don't want that thing*
anywhere near the baby, my husband says. When I look at him,
I only see the ghost. It is a bright heat that moves
through his body. It is painful to be unable to protect everyone
all the time. Like her father, when the baby is overtired,
her cheeks and ears glow unnaturally red.

The Sound of the Ghost

On the highway, the tires make the sound
of the dead over the cement panels
like a chorus of cellos. I feel it
in my body. The baby is lulled
to sleep by the vibrations. Does this
visit her there? Or is it only me
who wakes in the night, out of someone
else's dream? A place I have never been,
figures who almost coalesce,
conversation too quiet to hear.
My husband, in the morning, says:
*I know where you went, last night. Who you
were with.* I dip stale munchkins in my tea,
and the oil floats on the surface. *Remember,*
he says, *it isn't always easier to disappear.*

The Body I Had

In what dimension
do ghosts live? I rest
on the floor next to
the baby's library
and ask her to come sit
on my lap. She is too busy
learning, doing the things
that a baby must do,
to stop and sit with me.
I see through my body
to my heart when it skips
a beat. I see through me
to the past-me to the body
I had before my daughter.
I am the only one
that thinks my body now
is more beautiful.

The Ghost Sleeps

The ghost nestles in my daughter's neck;
in the other room, my husband sleeps.
I too wake with a crick in my shoulder
and a question in my mouth. The question
is sour, is purple, is something I used to know
the answer to. Because we are sick and sleep
all day, we draw the blinds.
A sinister tool cut an answer into the tender
flesh of my throat while I dreamed. I dreamed
of ice cream, of a baby who was taken apart
and reassembled. What is my brain
trying to tell me? Something I want to know?
Pain's purpose is finite; it would be better
for everyone if we could let it go.

The Ghost Is My Own

The ghost is my own making.
The neurologist clears me,
and yet the ghost remains. I think
irrational, irrational, irrational, as though
repeating this incantation will correct
the pathways in my brain. My therapist asks
about the ghost. Is it my father? Is it
the pain that wakes me
at night? I stroke the long fur of her cat
while trying to sort out this seed
of paralyzing fear that's choking
the healthy vegetation. My daughter sees
food turn to sand in my mouth.
Please don't remember.

The Baby Reaches for the Spoils

Panic fills the space between us
like a thick fog. All night I wake gasping
with the ghost holding me down.
Why can't I just relax and accept this?
I think of all the unsent emails to my father
being held in my drafts folder. Nothing
is really important. I think that's what he'd say
if he was here. My daughter's eyes
are the shape of my grandmother's. I squint at her
until her features are meaningless.
My thoughts defy gravity and yet
they are heavy with dark substance.
There are rules here. How do I reach
into the past in a productive way?
Whenever I do my hands come up filled
with shredded leaves, India ink,
and jumbled conversations. The baby
reaches for the spoils. One day perhaps
I can help her make sense of it.

Too Soon to Disappear

Washing dishes,
I notice my hands
losing opacity.
My daughter's curls
slip through my fingers.
I shake
so that the teacup
sloshes. Am I
becoming a ghost?
It's too soon
to disappear.

Since the Ghost

The ghost curls between me and my daughter,
warm as a cat, purring. We feel closer
to each other because of it. Looking
into the window, I can almost see
the reflection of our orbits: the shape
of a binary star, blurred movement.
We listen to lullabies as we do
every night. She is too young to know,
really know, about the ghost, but she sees
that it makes me lonely and climbs into
my lap from beside me on the couch.
Since this has come into our lives, fruit tastes
sweeter, cream is more cooling, and fear
the coldest icy vein of ore. My daughter's curls
are circles of fire. They burn my hand, my chest,
my cheek. I put my skin against them defiantly.

The Ghost's Hand

It is hard to say when I first noticed it. I think maybe
I felt it pressing against my organs as my daughter did.
I felt a hand during the Braxton Hicks contractions.
We had moved to the forest in the city. I wandered the paths
trying to become lost. But the low moan of the highway
was always audible. I glimpsed figures, sometimes,
in the fenced-off portion of the park below the disused train line,
but I could never find the opening in which they slipped through.
Looking harder: were those figures? Or were they dark, high stumps,
decomposing, making new life, housing a family of raccoons?

The Ghost Leaves Notes

The ghost leaves notes
on the fogged windows
like "love you" and "don't
forget." I never know
what I'm supposed to
remember. When it snows,
my thoughts are almost
corporeal. Like the cold
does something. In the city
everything is muffled:
the traffic, the above ground train,
my own rushing blood.
My period returned
the day of my daughter's
first birthday like a slap
in the face. Sometimes
it is my own emotional experience
that sublimates. Wouldn't we all
skip steps if we could? Even if
it makes the ending less satisfying?

I Catch a Shimmer

I begin seeing things
in reflective surfaces—
a shadow in the puddle
under the leaky faucet;
in the mirror that hangs
in the dining room;
in the lenses of
my husband's glasses;
in the earnest tears
of anger that pool
on my daughter's face.
When I look closely,
all I see is myself.
My mother says to me:
the metaphor is obvious.
Outside the air is heavy
with snow. My daughter
will call out the entire walk home:
snow, oh, oh, from the stroller.
She squeezes it tightly
with her fist until
it has run through her fingers.
She is distressed that
she cannot hold onto it.
The metaphor that
is so obvious
evades me. I am moving
fast. The reflections move with me.

The Ghost Wakes Me from a Nightmare:

My father was alive but sick—unable to speak,
like in the last few months of his life. He shuffled
from room to room with a walker getting smaller
and smaller until he disappeared. It is dark,
and my daughter's breathing is so loud
the baby monitor picks it up. Grief has found somewhere
to take root. I go to the window. The world outside
is lit glass. I let my skin become glass, too. I am
a ringing vessel. From here I can see the canopy of
the park. Bats tuck beneath the branches. The ghost
hears every creature living out there. I let it speak through me.

The Ghost Welcomes Us

Home after days of exile, my head is a balloon.
The baby has cried all her tears; she is wrung
out. Something has closed the windows,
and the apartment is cozy. The yellow lamp
in the reading corner is on. I'm sure I switched
it off. Books of poetry lay open on the desk.
This is where I found myself. In these pages;
in other women's voices. I read to my daughter
and she likes the musical sound. I trace
over the words that, like so many weapons,
opened up my adolescence. There is communion
in pain. It is what I needed. The baby's golden
eyelashes glitter with salt. One day, I hope,
she will find what she needs. It is something
we all have to do for ourselves. I know the ghost
is watching me lay her sleeping body
in the crib. I whisper, to the dark room: *Thank you.*

The Ghost Sees Beauty

The ghost sees beauty in everything:
the eyeliner stubs of my twenties, in jewel
tones, red lipsticks, broken, the box of bent
earrings I will never have time to fix,
that sweater that needs darning,
the sound of sirens up and down Woodhaven
Boulevard. My middle, which is soft and puckers
over my jeans. The black hairs that have appeared
in my hairline like dark omens. The ghost sees
all this, and still stays here with me. Collector
of things beautiful and broken.

The Ghost Pulls Tight

The ghost pulls tight the chords
in my throat until my voice
is grated ginger. The baby asks
for another story, so I try
to massage the ghost from my muscles.
Does she see me struggle? The ghost
keeps me honest. If friends ask how it's going,
I tell them. If the ghost were corporeal,
perhaps I would have a chance.
I sit awake at night counting
static spikes from the baby monitor
and question whether the ghost is real.
But I know it's real. I feel it.
My family has seen what it is capable of.

Rain on the Window

Rain on the window forms many tributaries.
In my own watery breast, locks open
to keep me from drowning. Now, with the baby,
there are many opportunities
to be pulled under or overtaken or dragged
down rapids I hadn't even known were there.
The baby's sleep is noisy, and I listen
for the loud gasps of air. Silence is the enemy
now that I'm a parent. I know that may always
be true. My sister's silence is still
a warning sign: something is very wrong.
I add to my worry journal: My mother,
my motherhood. My daughter, my daughterhood.
The baby sighs with exaggerated
contentedness in her sleep.

The Ghost Calls My Daughter

The ghost calls my daughter
from every object in the home.
That bookmark? A phone.
Her fork, too, or the wooden train.
She gets calls anytime anyplace
through any medium. She listens,
rapt, to the invisible voice
on the other end. Where is that end?
Running through my mother's house,
she stops to pick up an old recipe card.
Hello? She says.

What Attracted the Ghost

Though my daughter was born the same year
my father died, it doesn't occur to me
this is what attracted the ghost. Instead
I think of shiny objects like a rook might
bring to its nest: mother of pearl buttons,
hairpins, a lost charm, polished rocks or marbles.
My life has been strung together,
collected moments of pain and pleasure
and peace. The ghost holds these baubles
and weighs them. One the mass of a kidney
or liver. Another the weight of a toe.
My life is open for autopsy. *It isn't over yet*
I want to say. Am I convincing anyone?

How the Ghost Got In

It got in through the open window. On early morning
shafts of light. In the mourning dove's song. Up
the copper pipes and through the floorboards,
carried in particles from the radiator's steam. In my dreams.
In my husband's dreams; my daughter's dreams. It came
through the front door—it brought baggage and gifts,
secrets and stories. It came in the light of day
and under cover of night. Sometimes quietly,
sometimes with the clanging of backed up plumbing
or the harmony of lullaby. Sometimes with a chill,
sometimes with a fever. It arrived and kept on arriving.

The Amygdala Speaks for Me

The ghost teaches me about my brain.
Did I once know the amygdala
doesn't respond to reason?
I try to trick it with deep breathing,
muscle release, eventually chemicals.
For months I've been running on pure
adrenaline. I can't believe I'll ever be safe.

The Ghost's Demands

The ghost comes to me with a list of demands;
my body makes demands on me, too.
And the baby in the other room, her eyelashes
golden stitches, her hungry mouth full of need.
I have nowhere to go, but the ghost asks me
to leave. This is its first demand. I rise
from my bed, despite the leaden pain, and disappear
into the night. The cars along Woodhaven Boulevard
echo against the brick buildings as I swoop down
into the forest canopy and join the bats looking
for mosquitos and other flying insects. The ghost
did not ask me to transform, but it comes
as naturally as pain. As naturally as the milk
that leaks into my bra when I wake with stone
breasts. I'm tempted to stay here, a wild creature
of fur and wing, but the ghost is gentle but firm.
Would my family miss me? The ghost says yes.
The list of demands becomes dust—I try
to grab it, but it crumbles into motes. It was never
solid. Like my grief, it only held itself in shape.
The shape of grief or pain or the ghost is whatever
shape it needs to take. It could fill your world.
It could hide in the very atoms of your body.
I don't believe it will ever be gone.

Thank the Ghost

Going through the subway tunnels
I think of the ghost. Is death like
the interchanges? Many tracks
and switches in the dark, with work lights
on utility cords to illuminate the path?
A person could get lost there. The ghost found
its way to me with purpose. I cook
strong spices and turn up the heat. The apartment
is full of flavors and smoke. Our baby
babbles in the other room; dancing
with her hands held out. Sometimes it is only
that little girl who keeps me tethered.

Who Bends the Light

All light that enters
the apartment is filtered through
my compulsive behavior. When we signed
the closing papers, the ghost dried the ink.
What part of our lives really exists
when my fear is removed? My daughter learns
new words every day. She shapes her mouth
around the sounds. Vowel consonant vowel.
Language grows inside of her
like the roots of a garden. Who tends
this communication? Who bends the light
just so to land on "red" "purple" "green"?

Always Looking Somewhere

My daughter will never remember
my father. This is something that happens
for a lot of people, though that doesn't placate me.
The things that are important to me
and have shaped me and made me who I am
will be different for her. Sometimes at night,
I gaze at the baby monitor and feel the ghost
gazing back at me. We are always looking elsewhere:
into the past or the future. I want so desperately
to see the future that my daughter will imagine
for herself, and I want to know:
you will be there; you will survive.

The Ghost Transcends

The sensation is hot and cold;
this time the ghost transcends
temperature. My daughter cries
as I lay her down. I ask her what she dreams,
and she says *of my bed*. Mornings
when the sun rises, I am Grýla,
turning to stone. Heavy in limb
and regret. The body beside me
is wound as a watch, sure as
a mechanism—constant, dependable.
What makes it so hard to love
the body I'm in? Pain threads through
my muscle to remind me that
against all odds, I have lived
with this and live with it still.

Things That Happen Inside This Apartment

My husband and I wake at 3 a.m. to sleet
falling in our bedroom. Our emotional weather sticks
to our faces. There are a lot of things that happen
inside this apartment that go unseen. The baby's cars
roll under the couch; roaches, undetected, migrate
in the night, and I believe we are blissfully
pest-free. The ghost notices. In baby books,
experts say that before verbal communication,
children understand tone of voice. It must be true
for our baby who has started calling us
both by name. I am as often Emily
as Mama. I tell her *Yes, that is Mama's name.*
She lets us see her delight as much as her outrage.
On the baby monitor, she sleeps peacefully.
There is no storm in her nursery keeping her
awake. I reach my hand across the center
of the queen-sized bed.

Forget About the Ghost

The air gets warmer,
and my adrenaline slows.
Sometimes I catch the ghost
from the corner of my eye,
but I never see it straight on.
Have I ever actually seen
the ghost? My baby is almost two,
and she has a word for everything.
A leaf is a tree. At least that's what
she tells me. *Almost*, I say.

If she's ever seen the spiky green
shoots of crocus exiting the earth,
she won't remember. I repeat the word
crocus until it has no meaning.
Spring is just days away; the woods are full
of sand, color hasn't come yet. As if carried
on the wind, green will appear in dots,
then waves of tiny leaves unfurling.
My daughter will learn to love this season
and its impossible optimism.
It may be that she'll forget the ghost,
until one day she's perhaps a mother
herself, watching her own child,
feeling something just over her shoulder.

The Ghost Sulks

When my husband and I fight,
the ghost sulks in the bends
of the pipes, clanging or
hissing. We are terse and trade
passive-aggressive jabs. I peck
at the carcass of our disagreement
until there is nothing left. My husband
watches, fascinated. It is hard for me
to let things go. I don't want to decide
that we've stopped caring.
Outside, crows lift from the canopy
of Forest Park like one great wing,
like the idea of a bird. A shadow
creature made up of moving pieces.

The Ghost Hides

I clench my teeth when
we host visiting relatives.
I try to appear normal, but
we tell them that the ghost is a member
of our family. A haunting from the future.
The kettle whistles, and they say: *is that it?*
I don't think they're mocking us. No, we say.
That's the kettle. We drink tea and the leaves
float free in my cup from a tear in the bag.
The tea is scattered over the porcelain;
it's impossible to interpret,
even for the dead. I don't look
to the future in that way.
I just try to hold on.

I Have Grown into the Shape

I have grown into the shape
of negative space, while my fear
has flourished. In fact sometimes
I am not sure where my edges meet.
The baby swats my hands playfully
when I reach for her. The ghost extends
my embrace. It is the bridge
between us. For the first time, my daughter
played in the snow. Each step was wobbly,
tentative: I traveled through time
to her babyhood. It is strange to see her
without her steel assuredness.
There is delight in the uncertainty.

What You Need to Know

What you need to know is the ghost's name
and the ghost's purpose and why your husband
is so against the ghost and why the ghost
came here at all and whether the ghost
really loves you or just says it loves you
and how the ghost found you and why
your daughter sees it and when the ghost will leave
and what the ghost wants and *whether* the ghost
will leave. And what will be left.

The Ghost Is Making Decisions

I realize the ghost is making decisions
for me, and it is time to tell my husband.
Somehow this confession gives the ghost strength.
It has good intentions, I tell him, *sometimes.*
We are riding the subway, and I watch
the buildings outside the window blur
together. At times I see people inside,
a family tableau; more often the shiny body
of the train reflected. *Do you love it?*
my husband asks. If he is jealous,
it doesn't show. I don't know how to answer.
A pack of seagulls lands on the subway struts
at Broadway Junction, all touching down,
wings extended for balance and
drag simultaneously. I want
to be safe. Is this making me
unsafe? I have to admit
that safety is as real as I imagine it is.

Becoming the Ghost

Now that daylight savings has passed,
the sun is still high in the sky at my
worry-over-my-own-mortality
time of day. When the ghost is absent,
all I think about is becoming the ghost.
How many ways could I get there?
Family history. Family history. Family history.
From the floor the baby giggles; she has learned
how to stick and unstick primary colored blocks.
When it is time to tell her about death,
my husband will do that. Losing my father
has saturated my life. What do I
have left? Thin, brittle coats of eggshell,
easily crushed.

Firm Pressure

In the morning on the train
it is hard to believe wakefulness
was with me all night. Stations
move past like a sped-up video
and I think I see death on every
platform. I can't stop imagining my body
at the molecular level. What do my cells
look like? I can feel division within;
weakness, illness, something stopping me
from getting better. It is a heavy
blanket over me. A firm pressure.

I Tell Friends:

I'm just having a little nervous breakdown.
I tell my therapist: *I know this isn't real,*
but it feels very real. Every new day
is a day further from my father
yet closer to his disease. I don't want
to fall apart like that. The ghost is
an ever-present companion. I just got
this little toddler. I want to see
where she goes. I see the cliché
that I have become and somehow
that makes my fear stronger. How
did I never see the knife's edge
that is mental wellness? My body betrays me.
The fibromyalgia pain becomes something
more sinister: my father's ALS, cancer, terminal.
Surely this will end with my death.

The Weight I Carry

A bubble forms around me;
everyone feels the distance
between themselves and my body
distinctly. It is easy to step back, become removed,
and then start to disappear. My daughter tethers me,
a hot, glowing sun pulling me into orbit
with her strong gravity. The days are grey,
and I realize I didn't really know spring. It is always
grey like this and doesn't catch green until
we have suffered weeks of desperation. Why
did I think that overnight the world would bloom?
This pain arrived with apparent suddenness,
a grey and tepid neutrality buffering my life.
But was it really like that? I have become used to the ache;
the weight it gives to my life; the weight I carry.

How to Accept the Ghost

Distinguish between the upstairs neighbors
who are rambunctious and lively
and the sounds of your heart. The ghost will tell you
what it wants you to know—maybe not with words.
The ghost knows the secret of death that winds
amongst your organs, a prophecy
for the future. A shadow. Unrealized
but unavoidable. The ghost sees you at night
not sleeping, thinking only of your father and his
four months of grandfatherhood.
Beneath your grief is something more sinister
—more selfish: fear. Now that you have a daughter,
life feels more precious, something you want,
not to be wasted. At night you and the ghost incant the list
of risk-taking behavior that you regret:
Cigarettes, alcohol, diet sodas,
Red Bull; the near misses too: Fast cars
and winding roads, dark corners and the man
who could have overpowered you
but chose not to. Words hurled in anger,
thankfully not for the last time.
How to accept it? This is your life.
Stop looking for ways
for the ghost not to exist. It exists;
not only exists but thrives.

The Ghost Finds My Sewing Table

The ghost finds my sewing table
and, while I sleep, uses my thinnest needle
to stitch itself into me. I wake in pain
but the adrenaline helps propel me.
My muscles ache and rain beats against
the air conditioner. What have I been doing
all my life to never have felt pain
in this way? The baby sees me stretching
and throws herself over me;
now I am a stack of creatures: ghost, baby,
and me. It is hard to see myself as the collection
of nerves, cells, and bones that I am. I never think
about my daughter's biological components
this way. Inside of us is the movement
of a star system. Circles orbiting, bodies sometimes
colliding, everything expanding and
expanding more until it stops.

The Vibration of Panic

In Kelvingrove the two-story organ
plays hourly. I remember the feel
of it. A whole-body keening filling
my rib cage. This is what my pain has become:
the shadow on the moon, the tear
on my daughter's cheek, the vibration of
panic that moves through me, regularly,
like the organ in Glasgow. I didn't
know what kind of chain reaction
my father's death would set off within me.
I disappoint myself being so weak.

Morning Comes

Morning comes like it does
each day I am still alive—
with my fear holding me
to the bed so I don't
float away. It is unnerving
to feel so massive yet so
untethered simultaneously.
Over the baby monitor
my daughter sings *rain, rain,*
go away, though the sun glows
behind the blinds. How long
has she been awake singing
to no one, or maybe to something?
It isn't that the ghost has hurt me;
It isn't that anyone is hurting me.
I spread jam over toast and I hurt.
I pour the baby's milk over her
cereal while she eagerly
looks on, and I hurt. I feel loved;
I feel lucky or happy
or grateful, and I hurt.

The Electric Air

The baby picks up on
the electric air as I allow
the ghost in. She has felt the shock
of static and hesitates
before reaching out. I don't think
she's afraid. This has been our companion
this long season of sadness. I try
not to let my husband see
what is inside me. I act
normal. I force my muscles still;
it is hard to focus on what needs to be done.
The tulips on the table are open wider
than a tulip should be. Soon petals
will be on the floor. I won't let them
be thrown away, though they are dead,
wilted, listing at awkward angles.
I hope they disappear and I never know
what has happened to them.

Trying to Talk

Something is trying to talk
to us. In a matter of minutes,
two light bulbs in our apartment
blow out. Taking the baby to daycare
in the morning, the elevator
brings us down to a basement
that we had never seen before.
Concrete, work lights. I had given up
on trying to communicate;
everything is answered with new questions
or illogical leaps or symbolism.
I have had enough symbolism.
There are new holes in the fence
along the park—I ask the baby
who she thinks uses them.
She answers slant.

Becoming Visible Again

It seems my husband
did not notice me
disappearing. But now
that my edges are
becoming visible
again, and he can
distinguish me from
the space around me,
it is obvious
what he had begun
to consider normal.
My husband has never
reckoned with his mortality.
My daughter is too young;
she only has love
for everything until
the tears come. Life has
its own agenda.
There is no point
in speculating
as though we matter at all.

The Ghost's Departure

I prepare for its departure. Spring is here;
it has been here. I swept the clumps of pollen
and tree buds out of my corners.
The more time we spend outside
the less paranoid I feel. We all know it is time
for the ghost to leave—even the baby has taken
to shouting *bye-bye* at the empty apartment.
I don't want her to remember me
this way. Neither do I want to be erased.
I must stop conflating the ghost with my father.
Wishing my daughter to hold memories of him
will not make it so. We ride the carousel together.
She sits with her father on the bench, and I choose a horse
that moves up and down. She looks on with delight.
The faces of these wooden animals appear frozen
in motion: a lip curled back revealing white, white teeth.
Hair that mimics the breeze, taut muscles in the legs
and flank. Are my memories in motion? Are any of us?
I read a theory in which time is not motion
but another dimension that we can travel
up, down, backward, forward. A dimension that is still,
can be looked at from an outward vantage.
Even so, we are moving within it,
seemingly in one direction. No matter
how much I'd like to believe otherwise.

In the Edges

The mist gathers in the canopy of the park,
like the ghost in the edges of our apartment.
My worry dissipates every day the sun
lingers longer. Soon we won't think
of this at all. We will be too busy
with the water fountain and slides
and easy moods of summer. This taciturn baby
will know only joy. My husband and I
will look into each other's eyes,
and it will be with bright, clear, laser focus
that we say: *we were only ever happy*. And if
the ghost comes back, we will know it; we will welcome it;
it will sit with us in the evening. A traveler passing through.

Acknowledgments

"When the Ghost Speaks" previously appeared in *The Gateway Review*; "The Ghost Is Back" and "The Ghost Knows," previously appeared in *Gaze*; "Wake the Ghost," "I Held the Ghost," and "The Ghost Flies Low," previously appeared in *Coffin Bell*; "Forget About the Ghost" previously appeared in the *Poets of Queens Anthology*; "How the Ghost Got In" and "The Ghost Is Making Decisions" previously appeared in *Electric Literature*. "The Ghost's Departure" first appeared in *Cordite Review*; "What Attracted the Ghost," appeared first in *Artemis Journal*. "The Sound of the Ghost," first appeared with *NationalPoetryMonth.ca* (AngelHousePress, 2022). "The Electric Air," previously appeared in *Slant*. "The Baby Reaches for the Spoils" was first published in *Muddy River Poetry Review*.

I'd like to thank my friends and peers who gave crucial feedback on this manuscript and the poems within. Thanks to Jackie Sherbow, Monica Wendel, Diana Marie Delgado, and Jesse Cataldo for their close readings on the full work. Thanks also go to my cohort at the Office Hours Poetry Workshop, including Sarah Marie Sala, Laura Cresté, Linda Harris Dolan, Sophie Herron, Jen Levitt, Maddie Mori, Paco Márquez, and Noel Sikorski. To my friends in the QCA Artist Peer Circle, Micki Spiller, Christine Kandic Torres, Chris Kibler, Sherese Francis, and Becky Band Jain, thank you for your ongoing advice and support in navigating a career in the arts.

Thanks also to Dr. Ross Tangedal, Brett Hill, Grace Dahl, and the whole team at Cornerstone Press for believing in and supporting this manuscript. Sincere gratitude goes to the Bethany Arts Community for the time and space they provided to work on this manuscript during their poetry residency. Thanks especially to Raymond Carey and Sarah Karstaedt for providing the time and support and childcare needed to complete and edit this collection.

EMILY HOCKADAY's second full-length collection, *In a Body*, is forthcoming from Small Harbor Publishing. She has five chapbooks of poetry—*Beach Vocabulary, Space on Earth, What We Love and Will Not Give Up, Starting a Life*, and *Ophelia: A Botanist's Guide*. Her work has appeared in NPR's show *Radiolab* and in a number of literary journals including the *North American Review, Spoon River Poetry Review, West Wind Review*, and *Newtown Literary*. She works for the two science fiction magazines *Asimov's Science Fiction* and *Analog Science Fiction and Fact*. You can follow her on twitter @E_Hockaday.